Bernhard Johannes Schmidt

PLAINTEXT compact

The ASPERGER Syndrome

for School Assistants

Bernhard J. Schmidt

PLAINTEXT compact
The Asperger Syndrome
for School Assistants

ISBN: 978-3750416864

translated from
KLARTEXT kompakt
Das ASPERGER Syndrom für Schulbegleiter
© 2015 Bernhard J. Schmidt,
ISBN: 9783738645330

Production and Publishing:
BoD – Books on Demand, Norderstedt, Germany

Bibliographic information of the German National Library:
The German National Library lists this publication
in the German National Bibliography; detailed bibliographic
Data are available online at http://dnb.dnb.de.

Table of content

I. PREFACE

> *I would be – grant me this request –*
> *The third in your band!*
> Schiller „The Pledge"

According to the volumes "The Asperger syndrome - for parents" and "- for teachers" the third volume "- for school assistants" closes the circle concerning the school environment. The aim of the series is for the key players in this environment - parents, teachers and school assistants - to all be able to pull together on the same theoretical basis. This can minimize misunderstandings and facilitate the exchange. Only the good interaction of all involved in the "band" ensures optimal promotion of Asperger pupil.

As in the previous volumes, the essential knowledge for school assistance will be briefly and compactly presented again. The interested reader finds the scientific background as well as sources etc. in the books "Autistic and Society - An angry change of perspective" (see bibliography in the appendix) as well as on my homepage www.autismusberatung.info

II. INTRODUCTION

Would you accompany an exchange student from Japan - many questions would not even be asked. It would be immediately clear to everyone that the student comes from a different cultural background and has therefore learned different behaviors. So it is in Japan e.g. not usual to look the other in the eyes or to shake hands. In addition, the social behaviors in Japan are highly regulated and ritualized - and quite different from ours. Also everyone immediately suspects or notices that the Japanese student speaks another language and understands English only to a limited extent. All of this would be just as clear to everyone as the need for and kinds of help and support.

The Japanese student needs, one would quickly agree, an interpreter, who translates between English and Japanese students and teachers.

And the Japanese student needs a guide who will familiarize him with the peculiarities of our culture and will show him the jungle of unwritten rules of our socio-cultural environment.

Because of the obvious difference, no one would even think of seeing the Japanese student as handicapped or disturbed - he's just different. The communication problems exist on both sides. The Japanese student understands his teachers, classmates, and host parents as well or poorly as they understand him. Communication and interaction always happens between at least two parties. But what about autistic people? Why do they need accompaniment as a student even though they have normal to high intelligence?

Do they also speak a different language, though not so obviously? Aspergilian? And what is the difference between "Aspergilian" and the language of NT people (neurologically typical people), since both are very similar at first sight?

Do autistic people have another "culture"? Do they, like the Japanese student, simply have other and certainly not necessarily worse behaviors than those we normally use? What are other peculiarities of Asperger autistics that need to be considered?

And what follows?

So do Asperger autists also need one

- **Interpreter**,
- a **Guide** and additionally
- a **Bodyguard**?

Exactly with these three job titles one can describe the task field of a school assistant very well. Why this is and what the specific tasks are will be explained below.

III. DEVELOPMENTAL DISORDER ?

The autism spectrum, which includes Asperger syndrome, is categorized as "pervasive developmental disorder" in the diagnostic criteria.
But development is something dynamic and not something that is once set.
And development does not take place in a vacuum, but always in a socio-cultural environment.
Especially the school is for children and young people a central part of the socio-cultural environment and place of learning of cultural knowledge as well as group behavior. So the school plays a central role in the development of children and adolescents, regardless of whether they are autistic or not.
Even and especially at school, it is decided whether the autistic person's otherness, his own language and culture, leads to a developmental disorder and / or the development of a personality disorder or not.
The positive cooperation of parents, teachers and school assistants is the central prerequisite for a positive development of autistic people.

Two things are indispensable bases:

1.) The acceptance of the Asperger Autist with his own language and culture. (See also on the Internet: Gray & Attwood "Criteria for the Discovery of Aspie")

2.) Understanding the causes and reasons for the behavior of the Asperger's pupil and his particular perception.

IV. COMMUNICATION => INTERPRETER

Neurologically typical people and autistic people communicate differently. And not because of a different language. The nature and content of the communication differ.

1   NT communication

The results of social psychology are clear: NT people (neurologically typical people - not autistic) communicate to a great extent
unconscious - through facial expressions, gestures, posture.
But also by e.g. the modulation of the voice and the unconscious imitation of the behavior as well as synchronization with the movements of the partner.
Although NT people also consciously adapt to a group, as the social psychologists Sherif and Asch have shown earlier. But even unconsciously there is an adaptation and orientation about this unconscious communication.
The imitation of the behaviors of the group e.g. in the form of group fashion and group language, a special group definition function is used.

Yes, much of the NT communication (about 60 - 70%) serves as gossip and only the unconscious communication of sympathy, the hierarchy in the group, etc.

The "four pages of communication" by Schulz von Thun (see, for example, Wikipedia) are so unevenly pronounced in NT people. Only a comparatively small part is used for the transmission of factual information. The majority, on the other hand, is for (unconscious) group communication.

This unconscious communication and orientation to the group serves as an "autopilot".

Without conscious energy consuming conscious thinking and deciding, NT people are unconsciously oriented towards the group.

2   Asperger communication

Autists (and thus also your student, you accompany) communicate differently. Autistic people lack unconscious group communication. There is no imitation and synchronization with the group. It lacks the imitation of group modes and behaviors.

For autistic people the communication consists of 100% factual information! Schulz von Thun's "Four Sides of Communication" does not apply to autistics.

Communication has only one side - namely factual information. This often has two consequences

- misunderstandings
- Exclusion from the group due to lack of (unconscious) group customization

On the one hand, there are misunderstandings because autistics often communicate far less than NT people. The unconscious part of the group communication is gone - leaving the comparatively small part of the factual information. This reduced communication can be misunderstood as

- rejection
- lack of interest
- mental disability / restriction
- ...

On the other hand, autistics are often unable to filter out the small amount of factual information from the mass of unconscious group communication.

The Asperger student is concerned with the communication of NT people with this high amount of non-relevant information as well as you, as your Asperger student tells about his special interest.

For example, if your Asperger student's special interest is the railroad (which he tells you about), and because of the massive amount of factual information on all aspects of the railroad, they only understand it as a "train station". With the communication of 100% factual information, NT people are usually overwhelmed - just as autistic people are overwhelmed with communication of 60% -70% gossip, that is, not relevant information.

By contrast, the absence of unconscious group communication does not perceive the AS student as part of a group. NT people are unconsciously subject to very strong self-groups / outgroup discrimination (see, for example, Tajfel's "Minimal Group Paradigm"). The enthusiasm e.g. for football and especially for the "own" club is based on these own groups / foreign group distinction.

The advantage of the Japanese student is that, despite a different language and culture, he still has the unconscious group communication and thus an adaptation to the respective "own" group.

Over time, the Japanese student becomes part of a group and as a member perceived and accepted. This is not quite but almost impossible for the Asperger student due to the lack of unconscious group communication and thus adjustment difficulties.

The common consequence is exclusion, marginalization and bullying.

In addition, however, the Asperger student lacks the "autopilot", ie the unconscious orientation towards groups or their behavior. Without the "autopilot", which above all also functions as an "energy-saving mode", the Asperger student must orientate himself and decide on his own, consciously and energy-intensive. At around 25%, the active brain is one of the largest energy consumers in the human body!

The difference between NT and Asperger students lies in the presence or absence of unconscious group communication!

This leads to problems for Asperger pupils in terms of communication as well as orientation, increased energy consumption as well as anxiety and stress!
So it is already clear why Asperger students need, at least in the beginning, an interpreter, guide and bodyguard. But besides the lack of unconscious group communication, there is another difference between NT and Asperger's students - the sensory perception.

V. SENSORY PECULIARITIES

Autistic people perceive the world around them as well as themselves differently from NT people. In some areas, especially in external perception, there is often hypersensitivity. In internal perception, proprioception, on the other hand, there is often hyposensitivity, that is to say insensitivity. Both can have far-reaching consequences.

1 External perception

In the areas of external perception, such as seeing, hearing, smelling and feeling, hypersensitivity is often present. It lacks the filters that hide unpleasant and superfluous stimuli in NT people. This can lead to problems, especially in an environment characterized by severe overstimulation, such as school.

1.1 Seeing

According to studies, autistic people see much better, perceive the environment much more intensively and are able to detect interfering stimuli like e.g. do not automatically filter out the flickering of a neon tube.

Imagine the perception of your Asperger student as on a summer's day with a very bright sun that dazzles you. In addition the perception of all details of the environment including the disturbing as already mentioned flickering of a neon tube.

It is easy to understand that this vision is very strenuous and associated with a high energy consumption, but also with the danger of a strong distraction of, for example, the subject matter.

1.2   Hearing

Listening to autistic people is best compared to wearing a too loud hearing aid. On the one hand, this leads to a constant and sometimes painful over-stimulation and overload of perception. But the absence of the "party filter" is also known from hearing aids. This is the (unconscious) ability to filter out an interesting voice against the background noise. For example, the voice of the teacher against the background noise of a (loud) class.

1.3   Smelling

People involuntarily assume that all other people perceive the environment just as they do themselves. This does not apply to autistic people. Also, the sense of smell of autistics is often much more pronounced. For example, a mother of her Asperger's son reported that, after physical education, he was able to assign the remaining T-shirt to a classmate by smell alone. Unfortunately, the environment is full of unpleasant odors that can cause strong reactions. These include e.g. also perfumes, but of course sweat, rotten food ... If you Asperger students say the food smells rotten even though you smell nothing - it's better to believe it.

1.4   Sense

While sight, smell, and hearing aim at the distance, our largest sense organ, the skin, provides information about our immediate environment. It is the sense of touch (tactus) that underlies "tact" - not music or the observance of social conventions! For example, if an autist in the US answers the standard question "How are you?" not with "Thanks, very good!", as required by convention, but perhaps with "Could be worse." this has something to do with honesty rather than tact.
And also the skin feeling is often a strong hyper-sensitivity. Even light touches are perceived as unpleasant to painful.
Clothes that NT people can wear without any problems are a horror to many autistic people because they irritate

the skin. Problems that can result from this are, of course, all body contact activities, but also e.g. showers, because the impact of the drops of water on the head is perceived as painful.

2 Interoception

Internal perception often involves hyposensitivity or diminished perception. Here are three important areas for (school) everyday life:

2.1 Pain perception

The pain perception of Asperger pupil can be significantly reduced. This means that the statement "it does not hurt" does not necessarily mean that there is no injury / illness!

2.2 Temperature perception

The perception of the ambient temperature is often disturbed. Neither "too hot" nor "too cold" is perceived. For example, your Asperger student may freeze at 30 degrees in the shade, but not at -10 degrees Celsius. This naturally creates u.a. the danger of hypothermia.

2.3   Feeling hungry

The perception of hunger or satiety regulates food intake.
But also hunger and satiety may be disturbed in autistic
people. Often, especially by taking, for example, Ritalin
(methylphenidate), the hunger sensation is missing or is
severely limited. As a result, the Asperger student eats too
little, although he consumes a lot of energy due to the
lack of "energy-saving mode". The learning ability of a
student is highly dependent on a sufficient diet due to the
high energy consumption of the brain!
It may also affect the feeling of satiety, so that the
Asperger student just eats too much.
The knowledge of these sensory features makes the need
for a "bodyguard" very clear.
The (school) environment represents a much higher
burden / challenge for the Asperger student than for NT
pupils. But especially the school, and that is the central
point for the importance of the implementation of
inclusion, is a key area for the development also and
especially of Asperger pupils!
It is not withdrawal from the autistic or social exclusion
that leads to the development of a socially integrated,
contented personality. Even and especially the
confrontation with a more or less difficult socio-cultural

and sensory environment leads to the education not only in the sense of a curriculum, but also and especially of coping mechanisms.

VI. ANXIETY AND STRESS

Only a few hundred years ago and in a natural environment, anxiety and stress were and are important for survival. In a modern, technological affluent society, these are often superfluous, indeed harmful. Through constantly occurring stimuli, the body is put into a permanent state of excitement, which is no longer reduced by "flight or fight".

In addition, anxiety in NT people is overcome by unconscious group behavior, as social psychology has already established in the 60s of the last century.

For autistic people, anxiety and stress in a technological affluent society are a particular problem - and for several reasons.

First of all, because of the hypersensitivity of the perception, the body is put into a state of stress.

On the other hand, because autistic people can not participate in group anxiety management because of the lack of unconscious group communication.

Yes, anxiety and stress are the main problems and also causes of other disorders such as skin and gastrointestinal problems, anxiety disorders, social phobia ...

And without "autopilot" the behavior of the environment appears as unpredictable and often irrational to the

Asperger student - and not infrequently it is actually irrational, and appears obvious only to NT people - without them noticing the irrationality. As strange as the behavior of autistic people is on their environment, the behavior of their fellow human beings seems so peculiar to the autistic. To a not inconsiderable extent NT-people (neurologically typical people) behave unconsciously, group-dependent and irrational. This has repeatedly shown social psychology for decades.

VII.   OBJECTIVES OF SCHOOL ASSISTANCE

What are or can be the goals of school assistance? In my opinion, there are three:

1   Achieve learning goals

Of course, the achievement of the learning objectives is in the foreground. It is a visit to a school and not a club or something similar. And the normal to high intelligence of autistic people does not stand in the way of this goal. But the achievement of the learning objectives, the transfer or a corresponding degree alone is not enough. Another important aspect of attending school is participation in groups. It is precisely the autistic people who are present in public who often have doctorates. This often lacks a corresponding social personality development.

2   Group and class integration

For the development of their personality, people need a socio-cultural environment. In this arises e.g. the "common ground", the common communicative foundation, which among other things makes the

25

understanding of others, of jokes and allusions, satire and irony etc. possible in the first place. Supporting class integration should therefore be one of the key objectives, in addition to achieving learning goals.

3   Make yourself redundant

It should not be a paternalistic tutelage applied, but the ability of the Asperger pupil to learning processes are pursued. These should enable him then to participate in the class, to achieve the learning objectives, etc. Goals are thus the development of coping strategies in dealing with the environment, the perception of one's own person, the ability to orient oneself even without unconscious group communication ...
But this also means that one of the central goals of you (the school assistant) should be to make yourself redundant.

VIII.   PRACTICAL PART

What are the concrete consequences of what has been stated so far, what should be considered? How can and should the three areas of interpreter, guide and bodyguard be implemented?

1   Interpreter Autistic/World - World/Autistic

As a school assistant, you are the only person in constant contact with the Asperger student, of course, but also with his parents, teachers and classmates. So you are an important link between everyone involved.
An exchange between these actors should be respected and promoted by you.
It should not be made the mistake of believing that just because the Asperger student speaks English, he also communicates like everyone else and you can easily understand him.
But as with a Japanese student, so in the case of the Asperger student, the majority understand each other, but the problem lies in the exchange with the student. The focus of Asperger's students is to convey the world, the communication and the behavior of classmates and teachers. And that on the basis of a communication

WITH the Asperger student. Unfortunately, far too often people talk about and not with autistic people.

Communication with the Asperger student is only possible if his "battery" is full. If the burden of anxiety, stress, sensory overload, etc. is too great and the Asperger student "switches off", then it is too late for communication. Then only retreat and rest helps. The acute time of an occurring problem is therefore unsuitable for communication and especially for problem solving!

And from what has been said so far follows automatically that communication with the Asperger autistic should be as free as possible from gossip, from small talk, etc. For the Asperger pupil understands this only with difficulty - but will learn it with your help.

Above all, give your Asperger pupil clear feedback on his behavior. These clear responses replace the orientation of the unconscious group communication. Unfortunately, autistics often get either no, a false or delayed feedback. Say goodbye to the "Psycho Babbel". This has become (unfortunately attributable to Carl Rogers) an integral part of social / pedagogy. But an Asperger student can not do anything with this kind of communication. NT people

often perceive clear communication without gossip, without a high proportion of non-relevant information, as unfriendly. This does not apply to autistics.
Autists can and want to communicate - just do it differently. You will also get as clear and honest feedback from hardly anyone else as from your Asperger student.

2   Guide

Due to the lack of an "autopilot", the Asperger schoolboy's school and its structures are at first as unknown as a foreign port for a ship's captain. And as the captain needs a guide, so does the autist. And, to stay in this picture, the guide gives the necessary information to the captain, enabling him to safely drive the ship into the harbor. But the captain is and remains the captain.

And also like on a ship's bridge clear feedback and a short, concise language are necessary.
There is a need for guidance, which can be done both in terms of time, visually and organizational.
With your help, the Asperger student will learn this orientation as the captain learns to enter a then no longer foreign port.

3   Bodyguard

Due to the properties of autistic people described so far,
unfortunately, massive physical problems can also occur.
In order to avoid these physical problems, your Asperger
student literally needs you as a bodyguard. In order to
guide the Asperger student through the school in a
healthy and successful way, the following points are
important:

3.1   Reduction of anxiety and stress

As already described, anxiety and stress are among the
main problems of Asperger autistics. These can both
impair the learning success and lead to health problems.
The reduction of anxiety and stress is therefore to pay
special attention. And that, among other things, simply
because you are a reliable partner and guide of the
student. That the Asperger student can rely on you, trusts
you.

3.2   Attention to the sensory peculiarities

The hypersensitivity of the Asperger student may be
another source of problems. Be aware of disturbing

stimuli such as noise, flickering lights and lamps, ...
Avoid strong perfumes and deodorants and talk to the
Asperger student about his perception of the
environment.
The possible hyposensibility in the area of self-
perception, in turn, should also be taken into account by
you so that it is not, for example, Hypothermia occurs
because the Asperger student does not perceive the cold
to the extent necessary.

3.3   Sufficient nutrition / energy

Make sure your student is eating enough, so eat enough.
Autists consume a lot of energy due to the lack of energy-
saving mode. This must be supplied to the body. This is
the only way the Asperger student can successfully attend
classes.
Also note that the "battery" may be drained quickly. The
better the "charge control" works in the sense that the
battery does not go flat, the better and easier it will be for
the Asperger student to attend class and social
interactions.

3.4   Retreat option

Your Asperger student should have the option of retreating when the battery is empty, for example due to massive overstimulation. Then it requires a quiet room, in which the student withdraw and he can recharge his batteries. The goal should be to reduce the number and duration of retreats and to increase participation in social interactions, for example during the break.

3.5   Bullying

In social psychology, a distinction is made between in-group and out-group. So far, however, has been overlooked that there are people like Asperger autists who can not be assigned to either side. They are "no-group" because they lack unconscious group communication and interaction. Unfortunately, Asperger students are often victimized by bullying, as they can not perceive the group's unconscious rules and can not follow them. As a "bodyguard," watch for signs of such attacks on your Asperger student. And, if necessary, when it comes to exclusion, marginalization or attacks, tackle it together with the teachers. One common reason for the withdrawal of autistic individuals and the resulting personality development problems is the exclusion and rejection of groups.

No student should be a victim of bullying - but Asperger students are not only particularly sensitive because of the lack of unconscious group communication but unfortunately also very easy victims.

The rejection by and the exclusion from the group is not only more true perceived by autistics, they also harm in particular the personality development and the development of coping strategies.

More about bullying can be found in my book "The Asperger Syndrome - between Mobbing and Inclusion."

For your Asperger student, school is not only a means of obtaining a degree, but an essential place for its socio-emotional development!

IX. BIBLIOGRAPHY

Schmidt, Bernhard J. (2015/1): Autistic and Society. An angry Change of Perspective. Vol. I: **Understanding Autism**. Norderstedt: Books on Demand.

Schmidt, Bernhard J. (2015/2): Autistic and Society. An angry Change of Perspective. Vol. II: **Support for Autistic**? Norderstedt: Books on Demand.

Schmidt, Bernhard J. (2016): Plaintext compact. **The Asperger Syndrome – Between Bullying and Inclusion**. Norderstedt: Books on Demand.

Schmidt, Bernhard J.; Ganz, Andreas (2016): Plaintext compact: **The Asperger Syndrome - not only for Psychotherapists.** Norderstedt: Books on Demand.

Schmidt, Bernhard J.; Döhler, Christiane and Deniz (2018): **Autism – Sexuality – Relationships.** Norderstedt: Books on Demand.

Schmidt, Bernhard J. (2019/1): **Autism and the Refrigerator Mother Myth. A Rehabilitation of Bruno Bettelheim.** Norderstedt: Books on Demand.

Schmidt, Bernhard J. (2019/2): Plaintext compact. **The Asperger Syndrome – for Parents.** Norderstedt: Books on Demand.

Schmidt, Bernhard J. (2019/3): Plaintext compact. **The Asperger Syndrome – for Teachers.** Norderstedt: Books on Demand.

Schmidt, Bernhard J. (2019/4): Plaintext compact. **The Asperger Syndrome – for Physicians.** Norderstedt: Books on Demand.

Schmidt, Bernhard J. (2019/5): **Autism – Fight or Flight. New Perspectives on Challenging Behaviors.** Norderstedt: Books on Demand.